EVERYBODY LOVES STRIPES

ALEXANDRA FLINT & EMMA BAZILIAN

EVERYBODY LOVES STRIPES

DECORATING BETWEEN THE LINES

ALEXANDRA FLINT & EMMA BAZILIAN

SCHUMACHER

PERSIAN ART

CONTENTS

BAZAAR
Summer Travel
Summer Fashions

INTRODUCTION

There are very few things, either in the world of design or in the world more generally, that hold truly universal appeal. Stripes, however, are one of them, a fact that became clear to us in the course of producing this book. It seemed like every time we mentioned the project to someone—young or old, male or female, a staunch traditionalist or dedicated modernist—we'd get the same response: "I love stripes!"

So why, exactly, *does* everybody love stripes? Maybe it's their inherent orderliness, the way they lend structure and predictability to whatever they touch. Perhaps it's their timelessness, a concept that's become increasingly elusive in an age when trends are born and die in the blink of an eye. Certainly it's their versatility: There's no pattern, print, color, application, or style that doesn't "go" with stripes. Or maybe it's more emotional, something culturally ingrained in each of us: Stripes remind us of childhood, of summer vacation, of candy canes and circus tents. Stripes make us happy.

Understanding the power of stripes and the countless ways they can be applied to the spaces around us, we set out to gather a collection of interiors representing the best of the best, from over-the-top tented follies where stripes cover every surface to pared-back rooms where they're the supporting player. The talented designers behind them represent a wide range of styles, but all share an understanding of the magic that is created when line and color and material come together just so. They offer proof that stripes can be for anyone, anywhere. And who doesn't love that?

PART ONE

Stripes 101

142

A BRIEF HISTORY

For a pattern so unambiguously straightforward, the stripe has a remarkably complicated past. For the first thousand or so years of the common era, stripes were considered transgressive in the Western world, associated primarily with society's undesirables: criminals, heretics, prostitutes, lepers. (Like so many moral dictates, this can be attributed in part to the Bible, which proclaims in Leviticus 19:19, "Do not wear clothing woven of two kinds of material.") Slowly, as the medieval era progressed, stripes began to appear in less unfavorable contexts (especially heraldry), and by the 16th century, the stripe (primarily in vertical form) was embraced by the European elite as a mark of status and good taste, used to decorate opulent interiors and woven into waistcoats and gowns. (That a motif so beloved by royals was subsequently claimed by the revolutionaries seeking to overthrow them is just one of the many paradoxes in this story.) Today, the list of people we associate with stripes is as long and varied as the pattern's possible permutations: soldiers and sailors, artists and athletes, servants and prisoners, beachgoers and bankers. Stripes themselves might be inherently simple—merely a collection of lines, after all—but the power we give them is as limitless as our imagination.

GLOSSARY

CABANA
Also known as awning stripes, this wide-width variation is a favorite for outdoor applications.
Above: Beaufort Awning Stripe fabric

SERPENTINE
Composed of wavy, undulating lines, this unique stripe strays from the usual straight-and-narrow path.
Above: The Wave Velvet fabric by Miles Redd

VARIEGATED
Multiple widths—not necessarily in any particular order—make this imbalanced stripe stand out.
Above: Horizon Paperweave wallpaper

HICKORY
Heavy and hard-wearing, hickory cloth was a common material for turn-of-the-20th-century railroad workers' uniforms.
Above: Edie Stripe fabric

FLORAL
Botanical accents were a popular addition to striped fabrics during the European chintz craze of the 17th century.
Above: Ariana Floral Stripe fabric by Willliamsburg

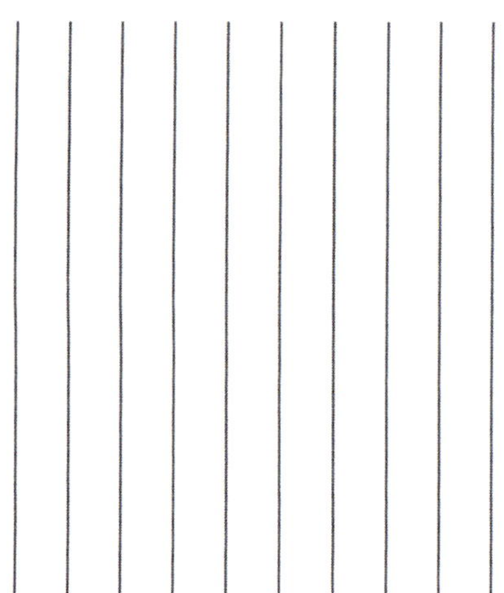

PENCIL
Approximately the width of a carpenter's pencil mark, these are slightly heavier than a pinstripe.
Above: Cavett Stripe fabric

BENGAL
A popular choice for shirting, this balanced striped fabric—generally white alternating with another color—originated in Calcutta, India.
Above: Tori Stripe Sheer fabric

STRIÉ
In the parlance of decorative painting, a strié is created by applying brush marks to a layer of decorative glaze.
Above: Gracie Solid Strié fabric by Mark D. Sikes

REGENCY
In 18th-century England, this balanced vertical stripe was a popular choice for walls and upholstery.
Above: Montebello Stripe fabric

BRETON

Named for its place of origin on France's Atlantic coast, the blue-and-white *marinière* was made part of the navy's official uniform in 1858.

Above: Brigitte Stripe fabric

TICKING

Traditionally woven in blue or red on a white background, this stripe was originally used as mattress covering.

Above: Antique Ticking Stripe fabric

BAYADERE

Indian in origin, the bayadere stripe is made up of colorful horizontal lines of varying widths.

Above: Kiawah Stripe fabric

SHADOW

Large stripes are flanked by thinner ones on either side to create the effect of a shadow.

Above: Rafe Stripe fabric by Veere Grenney

ROMAN

A rainbow's worth of colors—often in unequal widths—is key to this bold take on a vertical stripe.

Above: Ripple Hand Woven Stripe fabric by A Rum Fellow

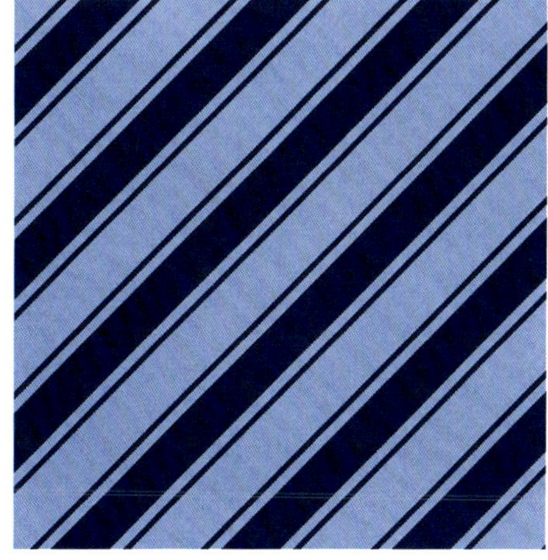

REGIMENTAL

Often seen on men's neckwear, the colors of these stripes originally corresponded to English military regiments.

Above: Tangier Stripe fabric by Johnson Hartig/Libertine

PINSTRIPE

In the early 19th century, the workplace of a London banker could be identified by the width between these narrow lines.

Above: Boyd Wool Pinstripe fabric by Patterson Flynn

RUGBY

The wide, horizontal striped shirts worn by rugby players still convey a distinctly sporty appeal.

Above: Baxter Stripe wallpaper

SEERSUCKER

Alternating lengths of tight and loose warp yarns are used to create this textile's signature puckered effect.

Above: Bailey Seersucker fabric

ALL PRODUCT BY SCHUMACHER

ICONIC INTERIORS

In 1825, King Friedrich Wilhelm III of Prussia gave his son, Crown Prince Friedrich Wilhelm, a Christmas gift: a parcel of land just southwest of Potsdam's Sanssouci Park. There, the Crown Prince built a small neoclassical palace, which he named Charlottenhof in honor of the property's former owner, Maria Charlotte von Gentzkow. Inside, architect Karl Friedrich Schinkel created a series of rooms including a guest chamber fashioned after a Roman general's tent, with blue-and-white striped walls, ceiling, and bed hangings. Two hundred years later, that "tent room" has achieved a level of social media stardom that most influencers could only dream of, not to mention status as a go-to reference for any designer worth their weight in ticking. (You'll see interpretations by Mark D. Sikes, Katie Ridder, and Bruce Budd within these pages.) Charlottenhof is just one example of the stripe's power to transcend eras, a fact well understood by greats like Elsie de Wolfe, Dorothy Draper, and Billy Baldwin, whose own legendary striped creations feel just as fresh today as they did when they were completed. Decorating trends might come and go, but stripes are always in style.

The Tent Room at Charlottenhof Palace in Potsdam, Germany, designed in 1829 by the architect Karl Friedrich Schinkel for Crown Prince Friedrich Wilhelm of Prussia, evokes the era's obsession with neoclassical style.

Charles Rennie Mackintosh's strikingly modern design for a guest bedroom in Northampton, England, was later reconstructed at Glasgow's Mackintosh House museum. OPPOSITE: Elsie de Wolfe covered the walls of the pavilion at her Villa Trianon with a fabric inspired by 18th-century France.

François Catroux turned a bedroom in his Paris apartment into an op-art masterpiece. OPPOSITE: Gio Ponti's Villa Planchart in Caracas, Venezuela, represented the height of modern design when it was completed in 1957.

Dorothy Draper's signature wide stripes set the backdrop at perhaps her most iconic project, the Greenbrier Hotel in West Virginia. OPPOSITE: Pink and white stripes reached peak sophistication in the loggia of Villa Verde, a David Hicks–designed home in Portugal.

At La Vigie, Karl Lagerfeld's villa on Monte Carlo Bay in Roquebrune-Cap-Martin, France, the legendary Chanel designer paired airy striped canvas with neoclassical furniture and art. OPPOSITE: The combination of a striped dhurrie with denim-slipcovered slipper chairs feels just as fresh today as it did when dreamed up by Billy Baldwin in the early 1970s.

PART TWO

Stripes by Style

COASTAL

AUDREY
HEPBURN
BREAKFAST
TIFFANY'S

Few motifs are as closely associated with a particular place as the stripe is with the sea. What began as a functional relationship—medieval ships hoisted striped sails as a means of long-distance identification, while 18th-century sailors wore striped garb to make them easier to spot if thrown overboard—eventually turned into an aesthetic one: By the late 19th century, European seaside towns were awash in striped tents and cabanas, bathing costumes and elegant fashions, all meant to convey a sense of escapism and ease. That connotation still holds true today: From classically nautical navy-and-white to the candy-colored cabana variety to naturally elegant wovens, stripes are a surefire shortcut to creating a vacation-ready vibe in any space, whether the nearest body of water is a roaring ocean or simply a backyard pool.

Red-and-white-striped art and pillows set the tone for the pool-adjacent sunroom in a Palm Beach home designed by Redd Kaihoi.

Amanda Lindroth used striped banquettes to provide laid-back seating at The Dunmore on Harbour Island. OPPOSITE: Tom Scheerer outfitted the pool bar at the Lyford Cay Club in the Bahamas with a sorbet color scheme that extends to the tented ceiling.

Hope Hill

Blue-and-white stripes in a variety of widths echo the sky's hue at Amanda Lindroth's home in the Bahamas.

Striped bed covers are a playful complement to GP&J Baker's classic Ferns print in a Maine bedroom by Tom Scheerer. OPPOSITE: David Netto used a striped sheer to add interest to a simple window shade in a Hamptons house.

A graphic navy-and-white rug grounds a sleepover-ready bunk room in Baja, Mexico, designed by Ken Fulk. OPPOSITE: Sporty red and yellow accents evoke nautical flags in Christian Liaigre's summer home on Île de Ré, France.

A striped dhurrie rug and white-slipcovered sofa provide a relaxed counterpoint to dark wood furniture in a historic Southampton home decorated by Tom Scheerer.

ECLECTIC

BALLETS RUSSES

Don't be fooled by the rigid lines and repetition: Stripes can be dynamic—and even a little bit chaotic (in the best possible way). Deployed at scale in high-contrast tones, they can create a dizzyingly op-art effect; rendered in a rainbow of bright hues, their circuslike quality comes bursting to life. It's no wonder that designers come back to stripes time and time again to add a jolt of unexpected energy to any interior, whether subtle (why not cover a low-slung sofa in a horizontal spectrum of hues?) or over-the-top (see the trompe l'oeil painted kitchen in the following pages for proof).

A statement-making sofa and multicolor ceiling beams are unexpected, energizing additions to the grand salon of Francis Sultana's 16th-century palace in Malta.

Haines Collection founder Jules Haines hung simple striped panels from curtain rods to create a pair of faux-canopied beds in her daughter's room. OPPOSITE: A cerulean and camel pairing makes for a cozy alternative to standard blue and white in this London sitting room by Sarah Brown.

ROALD DAHL
THE USBORNE ILLUSTRATED DICTIONARY OF SCIENCE
PAPER FLYERS
How the World Works
GUINNESS WORLD RECORDS 2019
GUINNESS WORLD RECORDS 2020
Nigel Slater
THE ROASTING TIN
SUPER BLEND ME! JASON VALE
JAMIE OLIVER jamie's italy
OTTOLENGHI FLAVOUR
SAVE with JAMIE
THE GOOD STUFF
NIGELLA EXPRESS
COOK with JAMIE
THE FRENCH MARKET
CAKES
BARBECUE BIBLE
THE TRAVEL BOOK
KAY'S ANATOMY ADAM KAY
KAY'S MARVELLOUS MEDICINE ADAM KAY
JOKES

Two different scales of stripe play in this Nicole Fuller–designed living room. OPPOSITE: A railroaded multicolor stripe takes the spotlight in a Los Angeles sunroom, which Redd Kaihoi filled with a mix of antique and modern pieces.

TRASIERRA
MATILDA'S 30th
COURTYARD
EAST
IS THE NEW
WEST
IS THE NEW
EAST

A fresh, simple stripe adds structure to an artful bedroom by Christina Nielsen. OPPOSITE: Fashion stylist Sarah Corbett-Winder shows her aptitude for pattern play in her London bathroom, covered in red-and-white stripes of every size and orientation.

A thin black-and-white striped sofa is the unsung hero of Nick Olsen's upstate New York living room, providing a neutral anchor for bold hues and playful shapes.

THE SIXTIES
ON THE EDGE
GREAT AMERICAN HOUSE

Vincent Darré's trompe l'oeil tented kitchen is a master class in transforming a hardworking room into a whimsical retreat. OPPOSITE: Painted stripes on the walls and ceiling of this Nicholas Obeid–designed space could make for a dizzying effect, but the tightly controlled palette keeps everything neatly in line.

Schumacher's Edwin Stripe wallpaper in an assortment of colors and widths fills wall panels to create a fantastical confection. OPPOSITE: Painterly striped fabric walls are a fitting backdrop for a sea captain's portrait in Martin Brudnizki's country home in Sussex, England.

RUSTIC

Among the words used to describe a stripe, "humble" is particularly evocative: It implies an emphasis on the hardworking over the decorative—think a simple mattress ticking, or a sturdy hickory-striped denim, or a handwoven rag rug. These stripes are natural accents for rustic interiors, adding just the right amount of verve to country farmhouses, mountainside retreats, and seaside cottages without overpowering their down-to-earth appeal. Extra credit goes to stripes that show the hand of the maker, embracing imperfection to create character that stands the test of time.

An earth-toned striped rug sets the scene for designer Thea Speke's country kitchen in England.

A vintage red and blue dhurrie plays up the Americana vibes in a kitchen by Hadley Wiggins. OPPOSITE: The classic buffalo check palette is reimagined in William Li's upstate New York home, where graphic patterned curtains are trimmed in a contrasting bias stripe and a vintage striped rug is tossed nonchalantly over the sofa; Schumacher's Isolde Stripe and Brimfield fabrics cover pillows.

In designer Lauren Weiss's ski-lodge living room, a ticking stripe adds interest to a grandly scaled sofa without overwhelming.

HOUSES
THERE AND BACK
RETREAT THE MODERN HOUSE IN NATURE

FROM LEFT: Isabella Worsley took treehouse living to new heights in her design for Wildhive Callow Hall, a hotel in England's Peak District. Alfredo Paredes chose an indoor-outdoor runner to withstand sandy feet in his family's beach house in Shelter Island, New York. A trio of blue-and-white stripes (including Schumacher's Jean Stripe on the chair and Nomad over the sofa seat) feels effortlessly at home alongside exposed wood and painted stone in photographer William Waldron's upstate New York home.

A window-seat cushion pays homage to vintage ticking-striped mattresses in a Connecticut home designed by Billy Cotton. OPPOSITE: Lauren Weiss used striped seat cushions to add inviting comfort to a wood-filled ski-house dining room.

BOHEMIAN

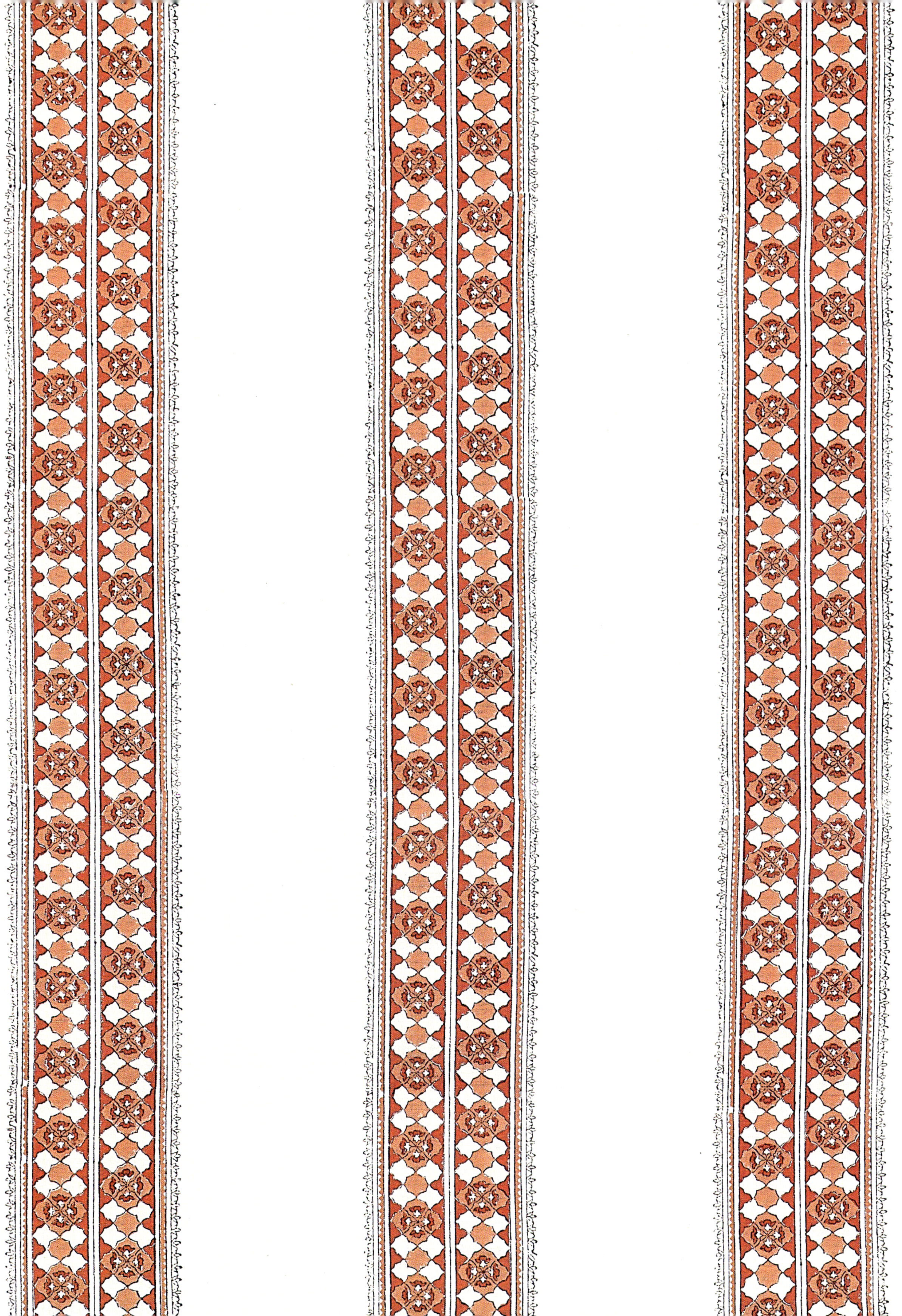

One of the greatest qualities of the stripe is its ability to multitask. Take, for instance, its pivotal role in a certain type of glamorously undone, globe-trotting interior. Added to a loose mix of ikats, paisleys, and florals, it lends just enough structure to keep things under control; as an accent to simple white slipcovered furniture, the stripe becomes an exclamation point, one that's more tossed-off than try-hard. The decorating equivalent of a barefoot contessa in a richly embroidered caftan, the bohemian stripe captures a certain worldly *je ne sais quoi* that's impossible to define yet instantly recognizable.

Stripes create a through line in Gavin Houghton's Tangier home; they're on full display in his sitting room, strewn across a tablecloth, fireplace surround, and painted ceiling.

In her home on Mallorca, antiquarian Amanda Pickett used a locally woven striped fabric to add panache to her laid-back living room. The antique gilded cornice tops it off in a grand gesture.

In the courtyard loggia of Veere Grenney's home in Tangier, a relaxed French box cushion is covered in the designer's Rafe stripe for Schumacher. OPPOSITE: Graphic striped pillows provide an essential accent for rumpled slipcovers and white plaster walls at the hotel Trasierra in Seville, Spain.

Ellen O'Neill proves that a strict black-and-white scheme can feel utterly relaxed in her Gramercy Park apartment, where pillows in Schumacher's Cabana Stripe top the twin loveseats.

Well-worn and well-collected are the mood in the late Min Hogg's sitting room, where a traditional stripe provides just the right amount of *je ne sais quoi*. OPPOSITE: Casually draped stripes add unparalleled ease to a formal canopy bed in Inès de la Fressange's Provençal hideaway.

A sheer, ruffled canopy offsets the stateliness of a 19th-century four-poster Portuguese bed in Frank de Biasi's Tangier bedroom. OPPOSITE: A true study in stripes, the bedroom of C&C Milano founder Piero Castellini Baldissera's home in Portofino, Italy, combines a variety of scales in a unifying palette of faded red and white.

MODERN

There's a reason why contemporary artists from Ellsworth Kelly to Sol LeWitt embraced the stripe: Its deceptively simple form conveys a bold, forward-thinking energy that no circle or square or abstract blotch can match. Similarly, stripes are an ideal partner for modern interiors, a sleek and streamlined complement to even the starkest spaces. Their graphic appeal shines in black and white, but packs even more of a punch in an attention-grabbing hue like lipstick red. And when a series of bold, straight lines is applied to a curvilinear piece of furniture, the effect is truly gallery-worthy.

A cozy wool rug grounds the study of an Ashe Leandro–designed ski house in Park City, Utah, picking up on the room's natural tones and textures.

A carefully placed wide-width stripe highlights the boxy silhouette of a sofa in a living room designed by Jacques Grange.

ASH NYC's signature Pillow Chair—shown here in the East Village apartment of the firm's former creative director Will Cooper—creates a playful tension between rigid stripe and soft form. OPPOSITE: The broken stripes of Schumacher's Maxwell fabric turn a simple roman shade into an attention-grabbing work of art in Benni Frowein's London bathroom.

A red-and-white stripe amplifies the voluptuous lines of Gaetano Pesce's iconic Up chair for B&B Italia, which takes pride of place in a Dubai home designed by Jafar Dajani. OPPOSITE: A dhurrie softens the brutalist concrete walls of Vincent Van Duysen's Antwerp home and helps delineate the seating area of the large, open space.

A custom sectional echoes the unusual angles of the living room in David Netto's hexagonal-shaped Hamptons home.

A graphic bedspread is a high-impact, low-lift addition to a moody-hued bedroom by Commune Design. OPPOSITE: Black and white stripes turn an undulating 20-foot sofa into an op-art installation in this Brooklyn living room designed by Somerset House.

CLASSIC

The definition of "good taste" is a notoriously fickle one: What's considered the height of elegance today might elicit a cringe just a few years from now. Stripes, however, remain a rare exception to the rule. While the preferred style of stripe may change, the stripe is forever. As such, it's an obvious choice for interiors that are meant to stand the test of time, whether the look is tried-and-true traditional (think Regency-striped silk curtains) or a new angle on an old favorite (like wall paneling reimagined in a variegated upholstered stripe, seen opposite). Classic stripes add structure without weight, creating a sophisticated backdrop that feels forever fresh.

Markham Roberts used striped red-and-white fabric to create a clever take on traditional wall paneling in a client's Nantucket dining room. The curtains are subtly trimmed in the same ticking, turned on the bias.

A breezy stripe plays up the angles of a cozy Charlottenhof Palace–inspired Houston guest room designed by Bruce Budd. OPPOSITE: Frank de Biasi makes the case for narrow blue-and-white ticking as an almost-solid, creating a strié-like effect on the walls of his New York bedroom.

A striped settee, rugs, and mirror are made to feel serene, not busy, thanks to Markham Roberts's choice of a neutral grounding scheme. OPPOSITE: Veere Grenney lined one of his signature box beds in a narrow striped fabric, providing a light counterpoint to the rich cashmere on the curtains and walls.

Carlo Scarpa
The complete works

Formal details like a crystal chandelier and stately mantel are offset by painted furniture, ticking-stripe upholstery, and hand-blocked striped wallpaper in this Veere Grenney–designed dining room. OPPOSITE: Studio Peregalli Sartori upped the old-world appeal of a Parisian bathroom with striped plaster walls that echo the patina of timeworn marble.

In a Park Avenue apartment by Brockschmidt & Coleman, walls in a rich turquoise-and-brown stripe have enough heft to handle the weight of serious antiques. OPPOSITE: At London boutique hotel Henry's House, a bathroom is enclosed by a Regency-striped "tent" (complete with tasseled trim) for a result that's both whimsical and sophisticated.

BRANDT NUDES
A New Perspective
Glamour of the Gods

Bold chocolate-and-cream stripes and billowing curtains with flouncy pleated trim make for a chic confection of a room in the hands of Miles Redd. OPPOSITE: A grass-green faux-bois patterned rug adds just the right amount of organic linearity to classic striped curtains and a skirted center table in designer Colette van den Thillart's London flat.

CHARMING

Interiors bearing a certain type of dainty stripe—think narrow seersucker or ticking, perhaps interspersed with flowers or trailing vines—can't help but convey a guileless charm that's hard to resist. The effect is multiplied when said stripe is applied to anything skirted, ruffled, or otherwise gathered. While naturally suited to children's rooms, the technique is by no means unsophisticated: Combined with moody tones and well-worn antiques, the charming stripe becomes a grown-up staple of country houses and seaside retreats.

Joy Moyler showcases the timeless appeal of a small-scale wallpaper with ticking-striped fabric in this petite bedroom, where the skirted bedspread and matching curtain (both in Schumacher's Antique Ticking Stripe) are trimmed with horizontal borders that highlight their graceful folds.

Florals and stripes play nice in the guest room of a 1920s Lake Michigan vacation house by Summer Thornton. OPPOSITE: Designer Allegra O. Eifler embraced coastal New England charm in her family's Cape Cod cottage, where heirloom furniture and antique quilts make a natural partner for old-fashioned ticking upholstery.

WHERE LAND MEETS SEA

A profusion of striped textiles adds to the collected feel of this Cape Cod bedroom by Allegra O. Eifler.

A voluminous striped Austrian shade adds a touch of circus-tent whimsy to a pretty floral-covered bathroom in Suffolk, England, by Virginia Howard. OPPOSITE: Libby Cameron used Kinnicutt wallpaper by Sister Parish Design as the backdrop for a pattern-filled Boston bedroom; a smaller-scale dotted stripe on the bedskirts adds an extra punch.

A palette of dusty hues tempers the sweetness of a Le Manach floral stripe and scalloped sheets in the former Hamptons home of Patrick McGrath and Reinaldo Leandro. OPPOSITE: Alison Newman took a similar approach in a Millbrook, New York, bathroom wrapped in Carleton V's Normandy Stripe wallpaper.

Botanical striped wallpaper by Adelphi Paper Hangings hugs the steep angles of this Hamptons guest room designed by Michelle R. Smith of Studio MRS, creating an almost tented effect.

PART THREE

Decorating with Stripes

WALLS

For centuries, humans have used stripes to create architectural trompe l'oeil. In the castles of medieval Europe, stripes were painted on the walls of great halls to visually compress the cavernous spaces; in the low-ceilinged rooms of Restoration-era Paris apartments, striped wallcoverings were meant to create the illusion of height. (Nowadays, it's mostly the latter strategy that prevails—very few of us have the need to reduce palatially sized rooms, after all.) In addition to orientation, there's scale and color to consider, but also material: Precisely painted lines might convey a crisp formality while an upholstered ticking feels cosseting and cozy; a multicolored array reads playful while a historic botanical striped paper creates period drama.

Painted stripes don't require a pristine canvas: At this house in Normandy, France, designer David Carter played up the perfectly imperfect appeal of plaster walls with a hand-painted design in a *tricolore* scheme.

An accent wall of upright stripes creates geometric contrast with a sinuously shaped chair in a London project by Russell Loughlan, founder of design studio The House on Dolphin Street. OPPOSITE: At his own house on the Kent coast, Loughlan filled a bedroom in hand-painted stripes; the darker ground near the ceiling helps draw the eye upward.

THE WAY WE LIVE WITH COLOUR
Valentine Warner THE GOOD TABLE
Art School

Thin blue-and-white stripes are always a fresh addition in a bath. Here, Salvesen Graham used them horizontally as the backdrop for sunshine yellow accents. OPPOSITE: Emma Ainscough went two for two in a country house bathroom, pairing striped wallpaper with coordinating shower tiles.

Soft tones provide a flattering background for an eaved bathroom in a 19th-century Greek Revival house designed by The 1818 Collective. OPPOSITE: Frédéric Méchiche chose pink and cream to create an airy bedroom that feels anything but brash for a chateau near Chantilly, France.

FROM LEFT: A Décors Barbares cotton printed fabric wraps the dining room of Markham Roberts and James Sansum's cottage on Puget Sound, providing a strong grounding force for a mix of weighty antiques and modern accents. In John Bossard's Atlanta apartment, Schumacher's Hydrangea Drape wallpaper provides a soft background for a mix of neoclassical furnishings, including a set of chairs in Atwood Épinglé, also by Schumacher. Peter Pennoyer Associates chose Schumacher's Le Castellet fabric as the backdrop for a Kips Bay Show House bedroom with a citron twist.

Using a linear wallpaper to break up a large expanse of wall space is a go-to strategy for Markham Roberts, who chose a brown-and-white serpentine ikat for this spacious hallway—accented, naturally, with more stripes. OPPOSITE: Madeleine Castaing's iconic Rayure Fleurie fabric is a favorite of designer Julien Devergnies, who used it to create a verdant oasis in his Brussels guest room.

CEILINGS

Sometimes, the most impactful canvas is right above your head. While creating a work worthy of the Sistine Chapel might be a tall order, a stripe-embellished ceiling is within easy reach. A simple painted stripe in high-contrast hues makes a transformative statement; for extra credit, join lines in the center for a mitered effect that creates a tent-like atmosphere. If the idea of creating perfectly straight lines at an unwieldy angle sounds too daunting, skip the brush and go for a striped wallpaper. More willing to embrace imperfection? Lean into the rustic mood of a wood ceiling by painting boards in alternating hues, or disguise a less-than-pristine plaster surface with loose stripes that show the artist's hand.

Sisters Olympia and Ariadne Irving leaned into vacation mode at their summer house in Portugal, painting stripes in different high-wattage hues on the ceilings of each bedroom.

MYKONOS MUSE

Miles Redd used a custom stripe wallpaper to create a high-style cabana in the foyer of a Southampton house. OPPOSITE: Designers Tali Roth and Tina Rich treated their office ceiling with a cheerful stripe for a graphic punch that serves as the room's focal point.

FROM LEFT: Striped wallpaper continues up across the ceiling in this room by Collins Interiors, meeting in the middle for a statement-making graphic effect. Marie-Anne Oudejans showcased the cross-cultural appeal of blue-and-white with a boho scheme at the Gem Palace in Jaipur, India. Painted stripes get the mitered treatment on the ceiling of an Andrew Howard–designed Florida home.

Molly Mahon painted the individual ceiling boards of this shepherd's hut in alternating hues drawn from her block-printed Marigold fabric for Schumacher. OPPOSITE: A similar strategy adds playful punch to William Waldron's country house.

Libertine founder Johnson Hartig's fearless approach to color is on full display in his Los Angeles home, where he painted a ceiling in a large-scale stripe fit for a carnival tent [illegible] Red-and-white striped upholstery and [illegible] create a sandwich effect in Ga[illegible]er sitting room; white w[illegible] room in between.

FLOORS

There's an inherently pleasing quality to seeing stripes underfoot. Maybe it's the sense of directionality, leading you down a hallway or up the stairs; maybe it's the way they highlight the width or length of a room or delineate a particular patch; maybe it's the way they provide a containing framework for everything else, like words on a lined notebook. Whether painted over the wood planks of a seaside cottage, woven into a colorful dhurrie, or tiled in marble or ceramic, stripes have the power to elevate any floor, no matter how minimalist or maximalist, buttoned-up or bohemian your taste may be.

Jennifer Vaughn Miller paired graphic floor and stair runners to punch up a narrow space in a San Francisco Victorian.

Bill Ingram painted stripes to draw the eye across the living room of his Birmingham cottage; allowing some bare wood to show through enhances the country flavor. OPPOSITE: A similar tactic exudes beachy elegance in Amelia Handegan's Folly Island, South Carolina, house; the undulating pattern in the center feels like a cross between a checkerboard and wavy stripe.

Dramatic scale meets vivid hue to create a refreshing foundation for Matthew Monroe Bees's antiques-filled showroom. OPPOSITE: Striped tiles add a graphic note to a Victorian bathroom designed by Studio Duggan.

The imperfect lines of a woven dhurrie in pool-blue hues counteracts the sharp angles of a grid-like art installation in a Billy Cotton–designed living room.

paris

FROM LEFT: The "green room" in Pierre Sauvage's French country cottage is grounded by gaily striped carpet from his own Casa Lopez. A black-and-white striped rug might seem an incongruous addition to a Palm Beach pink-and-green scheme, but Amanda Lindroth uses it to play up her guest room's '60s mod appeal. The rainbow hues of a rug in Soane Britain founder Lulu Lytle's London flat unify a range of boldly colored furnishings.

A chunky wool rug in cream and brown puts a worldly mix of ikats and modern art on a straight and narrow path in a living room designed by Timothy Whealon; the mitered round ottoman is a tried-and-true decorator detail.

UPHOLSTERY

While there's no surface that can't be improved by a smattering of stripes, upholstery offers a unique vehicle to take advantage of the form. From mitering to trimming, railroading to gathering, decorator-favorite fabric tricks have the ability to totally transform the trajectory of a stripe, softening straightforward rows or creating dynamic new geometries. Striped upholstery needn't always be the star of the show: The pattern plays a happy second fiddle to florals, paisleys, and geometrics, creating texture and interest that solids just can't muster.

Subtle pattern mixing is at play in this London townhouse designed by Nicola Harding, where a hint of check peeks out beneath bold ticking cushions on a pretty banquette.

Narrow nailhead-embellished tape creates a framing device for a banquette upholstered in Bindi Stripe by Molly Mahon for Schumacher in this breakfast nook designed by Anna Wooten. OPPOSITE: Shelley Johnstone upholstered both the walls and banquette in Brentwood Stripe by Mark D. Sikes for Schumacher, precisely placing the fabric to create lines that extend unbroken from floor to ceiling. The finishing touch? A simple striped tape along the crown molding.

A railroaded stripe adds an unexpected, graphic note to an antique settee in Elizabeth Mayhew's serene dining room—and picks up the palette of Schumacher's Le Castellet on the tablecloth. OPPOSITE: Daniel Romualdez tempered a blowsy floral—Pyne Hollyhock by Schumacher—with dining chairs in a crisp, smart stripe to make a timelessly pretty statement in an airy dining room.

Even a petite slipper chair can make an outsized statement when upholstered in a horizontal red-and-white stripe, as Tom Scheerer shows here. OPPOSITE: Scheerer again proves the power of railroading in a Bahamian guesthouse bedroom, where a multihued stripe runs horizontally to create a headboard that extends behind a pair of twin beds (and is repeated on the bedskirts below).

APOLLO
BELVEDERE

Octavia Dickinson pieced together panels of solid fabric to create the joyful rainbow of stripes on this skirted sofa; red piping adds extra zip. OPPOSITE: Flora Soames used her own striped fabrics in vibrant red and green colorways to add a jolt of energy to a stately antiques-filled room.

Walls, sofa, and a trio of mitered pillows in Flora Soames's Sifnos fabric combine to create a Mongiardino-style den. OPPOSITE: In his Bedford, New York, guesthouse, Stephen Sills framed a stripe-upholstered tufted headboard with a strip of the same fabric.

A vertical stripe plays up the towering height of the tufted headboard in Miles Redd's New York bedroom; the fabric continues up and across the canopy to create an ultraglamorous cocoon. OPPOSITE: Designer Stephan Eicker updated a pair of Gustavian chairs with a classic Claremont stripe, creating a tailored counterpoint to less-than-staid acid green walls.

TENTED

In 1799, Joséphine Bonaparte, taking advantage of her husband's absence on a long campaign in Egypt, purchased a run-down 17th-century manor house just west of Paris. (Napoleon reportedly thought it overpriced.) With the help of architects Charles Percier and Pierre François Léonard Fontaine, she decorated it in the height of Empire style, draping several chambers in floor-to-ceiling striped fabric to evoke the campaign tents used by Napoleon in his military conquests—and sparking a craze for tented rooms that continued well beyond her husband's reign. Of course, swathing a room in dozens of yards of fabric isn't the only way to do tenting: Handpainted murals and wallpaper can be deployed to similar effect. For a finishing flourish, a touch of trim goes a long way.

The Directoire obsession with all things tented is captured in the painted vestibule of Paris's Hôtel de Bourrienne, built in the late 18th century and recently restored to showcase its original beauty.

Renzo Mongiardino embraced the small footprint of a Milanese sitting room by turning it into a cozy tented jewel box. OPPOSITE: Mark D. Sikes put his own spin on Mongiardino's famous tented rooms at London's WOW!House designer showcase using Iksel's Safavid Reverie scenic wallpaper and Safavid Wide Stripe fabric, both available through Schumacher.

Chauncey Boothby proves that a tented room can be more serene than drama queen by sticking to a quiet palette of sophisticated neutrals. OPPOSITE: In the dining room of a circa-1890 house, Andrew Howard used fresh green striped wallpaper and cheerful cherry-colored gimp to play up the lines of the curved ceiling.

A trompe l'oeil tented ceiling and lemon tree mural bring a bit of the Mediterranean to New Orleans in the Elysian Bar at the ASH NYC–designed Hotel Peter and Paul. OPPOSITE: Miles Redd enlisted his go-to decorative painter Agustin Hurtado to transform a San Francisco hallway into a transporting work of art.

Bright red tape hides the seams and emphasizes the architecture of a stripe-wrapped dressing room and bath in Fermoie co-founder Tom Helme's English country retreat. OPPOSITE: Martin Brudnizki's flair for the dramatic is on full display in the guest room of his Sussex estate, where miles of passementerie (and a striking fabric-lined bed niche) take tenting to the next level.

Barrie Benson transformed Schumacher's Charlotte, North Carolina, boutique into an escapist reverie with tent-like curtains in Schumacher's Brigitte Stripe and Bird Tree wallpaper by Neisha Crosland.
OPPOSITE: Veere Grenney used his Rafe Stripe fabric for Schumacher to envelop a cozy bed nook in his Tangier home.

ON THE BIAS

MANNAHATT
ARTISTS LIVING WITH ART

Sometimes things need to go a little askew before they get interesting. Case in point: When turned on the bias, stripes of every sort can give a room a whole new angle. Deployed in large swaths across walls or ceilings, diagonal stripes make a dramatic statement; in the form of upholstery, they provide a refreshing visual jolt; in even the smallest doses on cushions or trim, they're an antidote for monotony. But don't just take it from us: These rooms prove that changing direction can be the answer in more ways than one.

When he couldn't find the perfect fabric for an antique chair, Miles Redd devised his own bias-striped textile by piecing together strips of peacock, tobacco, and celadon velvet.

John Stefanidis created a jolt of visual interest by using diagonally striped vintage Indonesian batik fabric on both upholstery and walls OPPOSITE: Bias stripes turn a sofa into a jubilant focal point in stylist Benjamin Reynaert's New York City living room.

GALERIE BEYELER BASEL
G Braque
JULI - SEPTEMBER 1968
PRIMERA
TEMPORADA
DE
TEATRO
DE
TIJUANA
SEPTIEMBRE
OCTUBRE
JANUARY 11, 2007 – FEB
SON
EW YORK

Heidi Caillier enlisted decorative painter James Mobley to paint a bias-stripe mural in a petite Brooklyn powder room, extending it across millwork and molding. OPPOSITE: Animal stripes in faded ochre add a subtle directional accent to an eclectic mix of furnishings in a Celerie Kemble–designed New York townhouse.

BLACK MOUNTAIN COLLEGE

Rita Konig's diagonal striped Ronnie fabric for Schumacher adds verve to a bohemian mix of prints, including her Olive wallpaper and a pillow in Terry paisley.

Anouska Hempel made clever use of scale and angle in devising the myriad striped elements that fill this graphically charged space. OPPOSITE: Sarah Bartholomew injected a sense of energy in this blue-and-white bedroom with a Les Indiennes fabric printed playfully askew.

Markham Roberts stenciled a wide diagonal stripe over solid grasscloth for a client's New York entry gallery, mirroring the design in the adjoining room.

ALL OVER

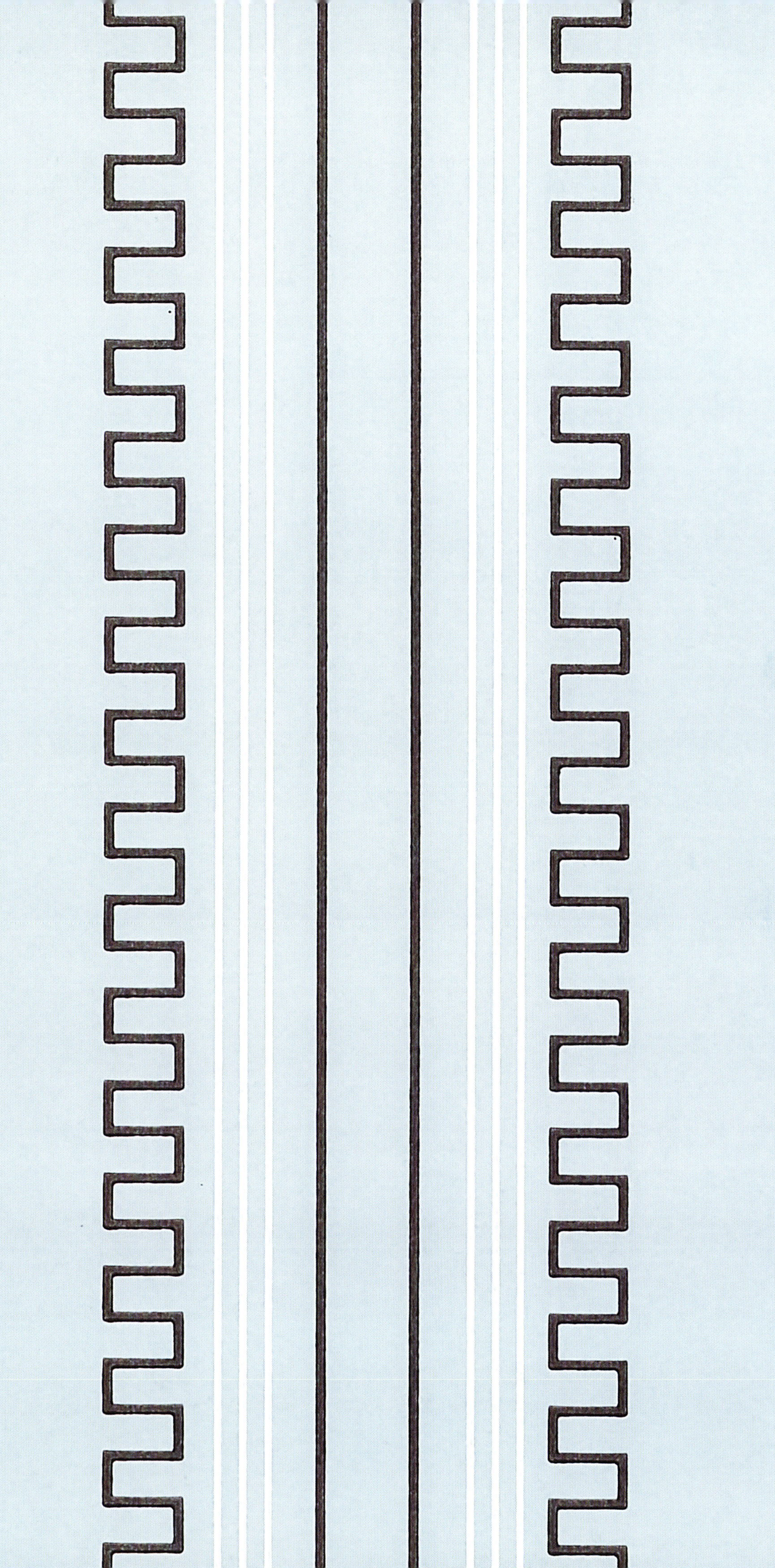

While a room dressed head to toe in stripes might sound like a one-way ticket to dizzyville, when deployed with a decorator's deft hand, the result can be anything but garish—not to mention an indispensable strategy for camouflaging awkward architecture or making the most of a small footprint. So what's the secret to making it work? First, create cohesion by sticking to a strict palette (but feel free to vary the scale and orientation of your chosen stripe). Second, consider placement: Align striped walls and upholstery with military precision to establish a sense of order, or place them intentionally off-kilter for a tossed-off effect. And finally, cut back on clutter to avoid chaos and really let your stripes shine.

Mark D. Sikes wrapped the guest room of a historic Beverly Hills estate in Fermoie's Tented Stripe to evoke Old Hollywood drama.

A pillow-filled bed nook wrapped in carnival stripes beckons visitors at the home of Pierre Frey chairman Patrick Frey and his wife, Lorraine. OPPOSITE: Red and white stripes feel simultaneously rustic and refined in the guest room of Emma Jane Pilkington's Greenwich, Connecticut, home.

Mark D. Sikes traded his signature blues and greens for quiet beige in his stripe-covered Los Angeles library-slash-guest-room.

Stripes extend from floor to ceiling—and even over crown molding—in Tom Scheerer's take on a tented Venetian palazzo bedroom. OPPOSITE: Antique textiles expert Christopher Moore used his Pompadour floral stripe—based on an 18th-century design—to fashion a period-perfect bedroom in a French chateau.

FROM LEFT: Sarah Sherman Samuel used her own Painterly Stripe fabric and matching wallpaper for a bedroom that exudes warmth even on the coldest Michigan days. It's hard to pick a focal point in this striped fantasy of a space devised by stylists Gabby Deeming and Ruth Sleightholme, but the slipcovered heart-shaped chairs—complete with pleated skirts—might take the cake. Wide cabana stripes in pool blue and tangerine ooze summertime style in a scheme dreamed up by table linens brand Summerill & Bishop.

Ashley Hicks and Martina Mondadori used Mark D. Sikes's Ojai Stripe fabric for Schumacher to create a cozy twin bedroom for the Cabana Bungalow at the Colony Hotel in Palm Beach. OPPOSITE: A bedroom at Thomas Jefferson's Monticello and the "tent room" at Charlottenhof Palace were the inspiration for this bedroom in the Millbrook, New York, home of Peter Pennoyer and Katie Ridder.

OUTDOORS

Beach cabanas, pool towels, patio umbrellas, swim trunks: Stripes have become synonymous with just about every accoutrement of outdoor living, evoking images of leisure, of fun, of fresh air and sun-drenched afternoons. The dominant variation, often referred to as an awning or cabana stripe, tends to be wide and almost always composed of a single hue paired with crisp white—a graphic, high-contrast statement that might seem overbearing when confined indoors but is just right against a backdrop of blue skies, lush lawns, or sandy shores.

At Veere Grenney's home in Tangier, a stripe-painted tin cabana protects al fresco diners from the heavy dew that rolls in after dark.

Mary McDonald had *My Fair Lady* on the mind when she dreamed up this striped loggia for a Tudor-style house in Los Angeles. OPPOSITE: It doesn't get more classic than the black-and-white striped awning that covers Timothy Whealon's terrace overlooking Gramercy Park (and provides shade for Ollie, his Canadian Ganaraskan).

A palette of blues unifies a cacophony of stripes at Sig Bergamin's beachside retreat in Brazil.

A red-and-white striped banquette, handpainted tiles, and iron lanterns evoke a Moroccan oasis at a Mark D. Sikes–designed Los Angeles home. OPPOSITE: Red striped chair cushions pop against a sea of zigzags and gingham at Gavin Houghton's Tangier home.

ACKNOWLEDGMENTS

We would like to extend our deepest gratitude to the following people:

Dara Caponigro for providing your insight, guidance, and encouragement at each step along the way.

Steph Diaz for your partnership, patience, and dedication to every aspect of this project. None of this would have been possible without you.

Timur Yumusaklar, F. Schumacher & Co.'s fearless leader who challenges us to forge our own path and open doors to new opportunities.

Jessica Tolmach for leading FSCO Books into ever more exciting territory.

Our wonderful partners at Monacelli and Phaidon for your expertise, advice, and direction as we continue to dive into the world of book publishing.

The Schumacher Design Studio and its many collaborators for creating the beautiful product featured throughout this book.

The talented designers whose incredible interiors never cease to amaze and delight.

The visionary photographers who bring these stunning projects to life.

The gracious homeowners who have shared their homes with us.

The entire F. Schumacher & Co. family for fostering a workplace filled with boundless creativity.

The Schumacher, Pozier, and Puschel families for your unmatchable stewardship of this company for more than 135 years.

The Schumacher Board of Directors for your leadership and guidance.

A NOTE FROM ALEXANDRA:

First and foremost, to Dara Caponigro, Emma Bazilian, and Stephanie Diaz—the absolute dream team. Working with you all on this book has been such a gift. For you all to believe in this idea and support bringing it to life—my gratitude knows no bounds! Dara, I am constantly inspired by your exceptional vision and incomparable eye. Emma, to have a partner in this book with your singular decorating point of view, brilliant writing, and refreshing wit, I am ever so grateful. Steph, perhaps our most important partner in this book, you are such a talent and your natural ability to translate our ideas to the page is a true art. Without your attention to detail, patience, and organization, this book would not have happened!

To my husband, Gaige Flint, you are my incredible partner and better half. I am beyond grateful for your unwavering support, love, and enduring patience. To my mom, my ultimate inspiration: How lucky am I to have the most stylish, inspiring mother in the world! To my dad, you are a rock in my life. Thank you for always being there. To my beautiful boys, Owen and Wilder, you have given new color to my world.

A NOTE FROM EMMA:

Alexandra, I can't thank you enough for allowing me to be your partner on this journey and trusting me to help bring your idea to life. You had me at "stripes!" Steph, in addition to being the world's best art director, you are also among its best humans. I am grateful every day for your friendship, your humor, your knowledge of important pop cultural touchstones, and your truly endless patience. Dara, working with you has been one of the greatest privileges imaginable. Your wisdom, creativity, and taste never cease to inspire me. To my husband, Eric, I love you even when your recently discovered interest in Breton-striped sweaters means I have to change my outfit. And to my family, thank you for always being my biggest fans.

CHAPTER OPENERS

STRIPES 101: *Brigitte Stripe fabric.* ICONIC INTERIORS: *Markie Stripe fabric by Mark D. Sikes for Schumacher.* STRIPES BY STYLE: *Audrey Stripe fabric.* COASTAL: *Lolland Linen Stripe fabric.* ECLECTIC: *Larivey Stripe fabric.* RUSTIC: *Mathis Ticking Stripe fabric.* BOHEMIAN: *Amira Hand Blocked Print fabric.* MODERN: *Deconstructed Stripe wallpaper by Miles Redd for Schumacher.* CLASSIC: *Coco Stripe fabric.* CHARMING: *Cabanon Stripe fabric.* DECORATING WITH STRIPES: *Acanthus Stripe wallpaper.* WALLS: *Edwin Stripe Wide wallpaper.* CEILINGS: *Opus wallpaper by David Oliver for Schumacher.* FLOORS: *Baxter Stripe wallpaper.* UPHOLSTERY: *Tangier Stripe fabric by Johnson Hartig/Libertine for Schumacher.* TENTED: *Kubilai's Tent wallpaper by Iksel Decorative Arts available through Schumacher.* ON THE BIAS: *Ronnie fabric by Rita Konig for Schumacher.* ALL OVER: *Greco Stripe wallpaper by Mary McDonald for Schumacher.* OUTDOORS: *Cabana Stripe Indoor/Outdoor fabric. All by Schumacher, fschumacher.com.*

PHOTOGRAPHY

Slim Aarons/Hulton Archive/Getty Images (P. 6) Melanie Acevedo (PP. 56, 166-167, 203) Edward Addeo (P. 194) Gieves Anderson/Trunk Archive (P. 54) Richard Avedon (P. 6) Alexandre Bailhache (P. 55) Cecil Beaton, Vogue, © Condé Nast (P. 10) Fernando Bengoechea (PP. 210-211, 217) Carlo Bollo/Alamy (P. 10) Henry Bourne (PP. 57, 195) Carmel Brantley (P. 225) Simon Brown (PP. 134, 141, 164) Max Burkhalter (PP. 52-53) Helen Cathcart (P. 66) Pascal Chevallier (P. 107) © Condé Nast (P. 24) François Coquerel (P. 6) Paul Costello (PP. 64-65, 69, 111) Roger Davies/OTTO (PP. 109, 153) Zach DeSart (P. 205) Courtesy of Octavia Dickinson (P. 179) Pieter Estersohn (PP. 33, 36) Artist: Frances Featherstone (P. 6) Miguel Flores-Vianna (P. 174) Craig Fordham (P. 6) Mark Anthony Fox (P. 46) Nicole Franzen (P. 136) Douglas Friedman/Trunk Archive (PP. 39, 97) Boz Gagovski/The Interior Archive (PP. 120, 221) Oberto Gili (PP. 4, 22) Tria Giovan (PP. 32, 34-35, 94-95) Sarah Griggs (P. 161) François Halard (PP. 25, 88-89, 92) Nelson Hancock (PP. 100, 138, 140) Christian Harder (P. 91) Album/Robert Harding/Adam Woolfitt (P. 6) Heidi Harris (P. 173) Dean Hearne (P. 189) Courtesy of Anouska Hempel (P. 209) Historical Picture Archive/Alamy (P. 10) Courtesy of Min Hogg Fabrics (P. 81) Horst P. Horst/Condé Nast via Getty Images (P. 21) Chris Horwood for Inigo (P. 133) Stephen Kent Johnson/OTTO (PP. 38, 68, 123, 162-163) Haris Kenjar (P. 204) Kevin Kerr (P. 200) Max Kim-Bee (PP. 159, 206-207, 230) Francesco Lagnese (PP. 30, 37, 74, 75, 76, 78-79, 90, 104, 138-139, 144, 149, 175, 176, 177, 180, 196, 220, 228) David A. Land/OTTO (P. 190) Guillaume de Laubier (P. 186) Erica Lennard (P. 80) Tim Lenz/OTTO (PP. 116, 118-119) Pernille Loof (P. 62) Russell Loughlan (P. 132) Mark Luscombe-Whyte/The Interior Archive (P. 93) Guy Marineau/Penske Media via Getty Images (P. 6) Paul Massey (P. 170) Aimée Mazzenga (P. 208) James McDonald (P. 182) Read McKendree/JBSA (P. 191) Metro-Goldwyn-Mayer, Inc. (P. 10) Pierre Michaud/Gamma-Rapho via Getty Images (P. 10) Antonio Monfreda/The Interior Archive (P. 188) Derry Moore (P. 19) James Mortimer/The Interior Archive (P. 130) Sean Myers/Trunk Archive (PP. 222-223) Amy Neunsinger (PP. 214, 218-219, 234) David Oliver (PP. 105, 106) Tom Parker (PP. 148-149) Isabel Parra/OTTO (PP. 124-125) Clément Pascal (P. 96) Daniel Peter (P. 222) Courtesy of Hotel Peter & Paul (P. 192) Eric Piasecki/OTTO (P. 224) Marshall/Popperfoto via Getty Images (P. 10) Richard Powers (P. 183) Michael Putland/Getty Images (P. 10) Paul Raeside/OTTO (P. 108) Laura Resen (P. 86) Luis Ridao (P. 6) Manu Rodriguez/Manufoto (P. 51) Celia Rogge (P. 16) Matthieu Salvaing (PP. 20, 82) Hector Sanchez (P. 160) Nick Sargent (P. 139) Annie Schlechter (PP. 23, 48, 72, 117, 152, 235) Nathan Schroder (P. 148) Fritz Von Der Schulenburg/The Interior Archive (P. 202) Alexandra Shamis (P. 181) Michael Sinclair (P. 60) Rachael Smith (P. 44) Chris Snook (P. 47) Courtesy of Soane (P. 165) René Stoeltie (PP. 6, 137) Victor Stonem (P. 2) Werner Straube (P. 172) © Tim Street-Porter (P. 231) Courtesy of Summerill & Bishop (P. 223) Trevor Tondro/OTTO (PP. 49, 193) Christian Torres (P. 146) Courtesy of Hotel Trasierra (P. 77) Chris Tubbs (P. 110) © Unique Homestays; property available to rent at www.uniquehomestays.com (P. 135) © The Hunterian, University of Glasgow (P. 18) Simon Upton/The Interior Archive (PP. 40-41, 102, 114, 178, 216, 232-233) Jonny Valiant (P. 121, 164-165) Frederic Vasseur/The Interior Archive (P. 83) Alicia Waite (P. 50) William Waldron/OTTO (PP. 67, 147, 150) Björn Wallander/OTTO (PP. 66-67, 103, 122) Simon Watson (P. 158) Sarah Weal (P. 151) Hadley Wiggins (P. 63) Brie Williams (PP. 156, 197)

COVER

Andy Stripe fabric by Schumacher

ENDPAPERS

Emma Stripe Narrow wallpaper and Rousseau Stripe fabric, both by Schumacher

ABOUT SCHUMACHER

Frederic Schumacher, our founder, was two steps ahead of everyone else when he established his shop in 1889 on Fifth Avenue in New York. When it came to interior decoration, he had the uncanny ability to predict what was coming next and had the gumption to act on it. His insatiable passion and quest for luxury are still part of who we are as a company today. With over 135 years of innovation under our belt, we're committed to design that transcends time and rises above the ordinary, and we remain unwaveringly devoted to beauty and quality.

First published in the United States in 2025 by Schumacher Books
Frederic Media
459 Broadway
New York, NY 10013

Distributed by Monacelli
A Phaidon Company
111 Broadway
New York, NY 10006

Everybody Loves Stripes: Decorating Between the Lines
by Alexandra Flint & Emma Bazilian

Authors: Alexandra Flint & Emma Bazilian
Art Director: Stephanie Diaz
Writer: Emma Bazilian
Editorial Director: Dara Caponigro
Publisher: Frederic Media

Printed in China
ISBN: 9781580937085

Library of Congress Control Number: 2025938458

Visit us online:
schumacher.com
instagram.com/schumacher1889
youtube.com/schumacher1889
pinterest.com/schumacher1889